This Belongs to
The One and Only

....
(Name)

....
(Contact Number)

....
....
....
(Address)

Visit our website

www.megumilab.com

and find us on Instagram

@megumilab

DESIGNED IN TOKYO

Fuck This Shit - A Gratitude Journal For Tired-Ass Humans
©Copyright 2019 MEGUMI LAB - All rights reserved.

-Christy Ann Martine

When your world moves too fast
and you lose yourself in the chaos,
introduce yourself
to each color of the sunset.

Reacquaint yourself with the
earth beneath your feet.
Thank the air that surrounds you
with every breath you take.
Find yourself in the appreciation of life.

📅 Date:

😵 Asshole of the day:

🧘 I am grateful for:

😎 Today, I am proud I didn't:

😃 Amazing shit that happened today:

My Goals

🚀 **Goal #1**

_____

_____

Why do I want it?

_____

_____

_____

~ Milestones ~

Day 30

_____

Day 60

_____

Day 100

_____

My critical first steps...

1. _____

2. _____

3. _____

 Date:

☀ Daily affirmation - I am fucking:

🧘 I am grateful for:

😎 Things I did for myself today:

😃 Amazing shit that happened today:

The trouble with not having a goal is that you can spend your life running up and down the field and never score.

~ Bill Copeland

Goal #2

_____

_____

Why do I want it?

_____

_____

_____

~ Milestones ~

Day 30

_____

Day 60

_____

Day 100

_____

My critical first steps...

1. _____

2. _____

3. _____

📅 Date:

😜 Asshole of the day:

🧘 I am grateful for:

😎 Today, I am proud I didn't:

😃 Amazing shit that happened today:

Goal #3

_____

_____

Why do I want it?

_____

_____

_____

~ Milestones ~

Day 30

_____

Day 60

_____

Day 100

_____

My critical first steps…

1. _____

2. _____

3. _____

 **Date:**

☀ **Daily affirmation - I am fucking:**

🧘 **I am grateful for:**

😎 **Things I did for myself today:**

😃 **Amazing shit that happened today:**

What's My Greatest Superpower?

List 3 things that you are really good at.
How did you become good at them?

📅 Date:

😛 Asshole of the day:

🧘 I am grateful for:

😎 Today, I am proud I didn't:

😃 Amazing shit that happened today:

THERE

is good in everything,

IF ONLY WE

LOOK FOR

IT

-Laura Ingalls

Wilder

 **Date:**

☀ **Daily affirmation - I am fucking:**

🧘 **I am grateful for:**

😎 **Things I did for myself today:**

😃 **Amazing shit that happened today:**

I stand in awe of my body

Henry David Thoreau

Don't let your mind bully your body. List three aspects of your body that you love and why you are grateful for them!

📅 Date:

😜 Asshole of the day:

🧘 I am grateful for:

😎 Today, I am proud I didn't:

😃 Amazing shit that happened today:

What are the things
that you should

be **proud** of?

praise yourself?

How can you

celebrate?

reward yourself?

📅 Date:

☀️ Daily affirmation - I am fucking:

🧘 I am grateful for:

😎 Things I did for myself today:

😃 Amazing shit that happened today:

Scribble your heart out

Scribble out all your pain, self-doubt, and fear!

📅 Date:

🤪 Asshole of the day:

🧘 I am grateful for:

😎 Today, I am proud
I didn't:

😃 Amazing shit that
happened today:

You are a bad ass

Glue in a photo of
yourself that you dislike

Check every one of the boxes below to remind yourself of what a fucking
bad ass you are. If you don't think the phrases are true, ask yourself
why. Then, decide if you want to make changes (or not).

☐ I am fucking talented   ☐ I am fucking loved

☐ I am fucking beautiful   ☐ I am fucking loving

☐ I am fucking strong   ☐ I am fucking thoughtful

☐ I am fucking amazing   ☐ I am fucking resilient

☐ I am fucking smart   ☐ I am fucking exceptional

☐ I am fucking kind   ☐ I am fucking _____

☐ I am fucking rich   ☐ I am fucking _____

☐ I am fucking gifted   ☐ I am fucking _____

☐ I am fucking blessed   ☐ I am fucking discipline

 Date:

☀ Daily affirmation - I am fucking:

🧘 I am grateful for:

😎 Things I did for myself today:

😃 Amazing shit that happened today:

The Unthankful Heart Discovers No Mercies; But The Thankful Heart Will Find, In Every Hour, Some Heavenly Blessings.

— Henry Ward Beecher

📅 Date:

😜 Asshole of the day:

🧘 I am grateful for:

😎 Today, I am proud I didn't:

😃 Amazing shit that happened today:

SHIT

HAPPENS

draw some shit here

When life gives you shit, flush it away

📅 Date:

☀ Daily affirmation - I am fucking:

🧘 I am grateful for:

😎 Things I did for myself today:

😃 Amazing shit that happened today:

Things I want to say to my co-workers but I can't

SOME PEOPLE JUST NEED A HIGH-FIVE IN THE FACE, WITH A CHAIR

📅 Date:

🤪 Asshole of the day:

🧘 I am grateful for:

😎 Today, I am proud
I didn't :

😃 Amazing shit that
happened today:

We write things that we can't
say out loud. Because the things
we feel the most are hard to explain.

Write down 3 things that you can't say out loud.

AHHHHHH!!!

No judgement

Fuck all the rules

embrace the beauty of your uniqueness

Reflect on your emotions or thoughts

"The creative process involved in the
making of art is healing
and life enhancing"

~American Art Therapy Association

Draw an important childhood memory.
Now try it again with your
non-dominant hand.

 **Date:**

☀ **Daily affirmation - I am fucking:**

🧘 **I am grateful for:**

😎 **Things I did for myself today:**

😀 **Amazing shit that happened today:**

ood Enough

My son, beware of "good enough,"
It isn't made of sterling stuff;
It's something any man can do,
It marks the many from the few,
It has not merit to the eye,
It's something any man can buy,
Its name is but a sham and bluff,
For it is never "good enough."

With "good enough" the shirkers stop
In every factory and shop;
With "good enough" the failures rest
And lose to men who give their best;
With "good enough" the car breaks down
And men fall short of high renown.
My son, remember and be wise
In "good enough" disaster lies.

With "good enough" have ships been wrecked,
The forward march of armies checked,
Great buildings burned and fortunes lost;
Nor can the world compute the cost
In life and money it has paid
Because at "good enough" men stayed.
Who stops at "good enough" shall find
Success has left him far behind.

There is no "good enough" that's short
Of what you can do and ought.
The flaw which may escape the eye
And temporarily get by,
Shall weaken under the strain
And wreck the ship or car or train.
For this is true of men and stuff—
Only the best is "good enough."

Edgar A. Guest

📅 Date:

🤢 Asshole of the day:

🧘 I am grateful for:

😎 Today, I am proud I didn't:

😃 Amazing shit that happened today:

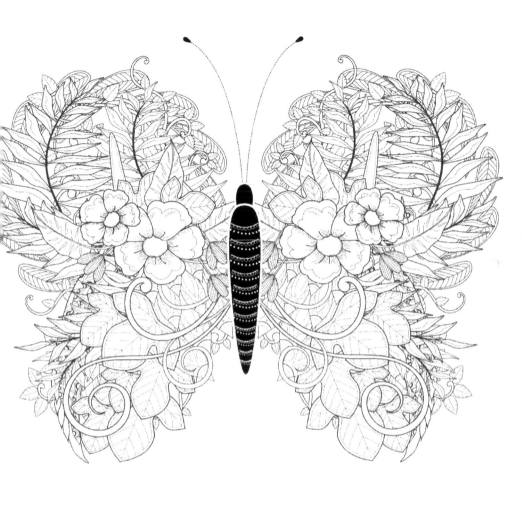

KEEP CALM AND

color on

♡×♡×♡×♡×♡×♡×♡×♡×♡×♡×♡×♡×

📅 Date:

☀ Daily affirmation - I am fucking:

🧘 I am grateful for:

😎 Things I did for myself today:

😃 Amazing shit that happened today:

List a few
things that make
you feel worry and anxious.
Then, write out all the worst things
that could happen and if they
happen what can I do to
get back to normal as
fast as possible?

Realize that most of the time
this whole story I created myself
is just nonsense and exaggerated

📅 **Date:**

🤪 **Asshole of the day:**

🧘 **I am grateful for:**

😎 **Today, I am proud I didn't :**

😃 **Amazing shit that happened today:**

If you could travel backward through time, what would you write to your younger self?

Dear younger me:

📅 Date:

☀ Daily affirmation - I am fucking:

🧘 I am grateful for:

😎 Things I did for myself today:

😃 Amazing shit that happened today:

To those fuckers

who have hurt you:

Rage page

📅 Date:

😜 Asshole of the day:

🧘 I am grateful for:

😎 Today, I am proud
I didn't :

😃 Amazing shit that
happened today:

THE WOUND
IS THE PLACE WHERE

the light enters

YOU

-RUMI

📅 Date:

☀ Daily affirmation - I am fucking:

🧘 I am grateful for:

😎 Things I did for myself today:

😃 Amazing shit that happened today:

Letting go

What are the things that you need to let go? What makes you frustrated, inadequate and insecure?

– Deepak Chopra –

In the process of letting Go, you will lose many things from the past, but you will find yourself

📅 Date:

😛 Asshole of the day:

🧘 I am grateful for:

😎 Today, I am proud
I didn't:

😃 Amazing shit that
happened today:

Document a boring event and all the reasons why you are grateful it in details...

_____
_____
_____
_____
_____
_____
_____
_____
_____
_____
_____
_____
_____
_____
_____
_____

Be grateful.

Appreciate what you have.

It's the little things in life that matter the most.

Nature's beauty is a gift that cultivates appreciation and gratitude.

~Louie Schwartzberg

Go outside

Focus on the clouds, breeze or trees

Close your eyes, take a deep breath and fill your
heart with tremendous gratitude

How do you feel? Write it down!

📅🕐 Date:

☀ Daily affirmation - I am fucking:

🧘 I am grateful for:

😎 Things I did for myself today:

😀 Amazing shit that happened today:

Remember yourself as a child?

What are the things that you desired so much, and you are having them now?

"Do not spoil what you have by desiring what you do not have. Remember that what you now have was once among the things you only hoped for."

~Epicurus

📆 Date:

🤪 Asshole of the day:

🧘 I am grateful for:

😎 Today, I am proud
I didn't :

😃 Amazing shit that
happened today:

☼ Date:

☀ Daily affirmation - I am fucking:

🧘 I am grateful for:

😎 Things I did for myself today:

😃 Amazing shit that happened today:

What are all the negative thoughts that you keep on saying to yourself?

Tell the negative committee that meets inside
your head to sit down and shut up
~Ann Bradford

📅 Date:

🤪 Asshole of the day:

🧘 I am grateful for:

😎 Today, I am proud
I didn't :

😃 Amazing shit that
happened today:

~Lao Tzu~
To a mind that is still.
The whole universe
surrenders

Breathe in and exhale deeply ten times

Let your mind clear

Start your day

If you have all the money and skills in the world, what are the 5 things that you would like to do/achieve in the next 10 years?

📅 Date:

☀ Daily affirmation - I am fucking:

🧘 I am grateful for:

😎 Things I did for myself today:

😃 Amazing shit that happened today:

Smile from your heat and
take a new start
~Kinjal

Write down three thoughts
that always bring a smile to your face

📅 **Date:**

🤪 **Asshole of the day:**

🧘 **I am grateful for:**

😎 **Today, I am proud I didn't:**

😃 **Amazing shit that happened today:**

WITHOUT GRATITUDE

AND APPRECIATION
FOR WHAT YOU

  ALREADY HAVE,

YOU'LL NEVER KNOW
TRUE FULFILLMENT
-TONY ROBBINS

>>>> ··♡·· <<<<

📅🕐 Date:

☀ Daily affirmation - I am fucking:

🧘 I am grateful for:

😎 Things I did for myself today:

😀 Amazing shit that happened today:

MY SUCCESS PAGE

Write down 10 things that you have achieved against all odds from the day you were born!

Remember them & remind
yourself when life gets hard

📅 Date:

🤪 Asshole of the day:

🧘 I am grateful for:

😎 Today, I am proud I didn't:

😃 Amazing shit that happened today:

you have good thoughts, they will shine out of
our face a like sun beams and
ou will always look lovely
Roald Dahl

Flood this page with good thoughts

Inspire others by sharing your
thoughts on social media with the
hashtags #fuckthisshitjournal
#goodthoughts

📅🕐 Date:

☀ Daily affirmation - I am fucking:

🧘 I am grateful for:

😎 Things I did for myself today:

😃 Amazing shit that happened today:

Write down 3 things that make you feel like crap!

Then, on top of those crappy things, use markers to write the opposite things, thing that make you feel beautiful, good & confident

📅 Date:

🤪 Asshole of the day:

🧘 I am grateful for:

😎 Today, I am proud
I didn't:

😃 Amazing shit that
happened today:

The capacity to learn
is a gift; the ability
to learn is a skill;
the willingness to
learn is a choice

-Brian Herbert

What have you learned?
and how does it
make you feel?

Dedicate today
to learning something new!

📅🕐 Date:

☀ Daily affirmation - I am fucking:

🧘 I am grateful for:

😎 Things I did for myself today:

😃 Amazing shit that happened today:

THE MORE GRATEFUL I
am, the more beauty
I see
-MARY DAVIS

📅 Date:

🤪 Asshole of the day:

🧘 I am grateful for:

😎 Today, I am proud
I didn't :

😃 Amazing shit that
happened today:

Morning ritual

Almost every successful person has their own morning ritual!
How does your morning ritual look like?
Remember to start small,
be consistent and,
reward yourself!

We are what we repeatedly do.
Excellence, then is not
an act, but a habit.
-Aristotle

📅 Date:

☀ Daily affirmation - I am fucking:

🧘 I am grateful for:

😎 Things I did for myself today:

😀 Amazing shit that happened today:

Fear	Results *from doing it*	Action

~ Anais Nin ~
Life shrinks or expands
in proportion one's courage

📅 Date:

🤪 Asshole of the day:

🧘 I am grateful for:

😎 Today, I am proud I didn't :

😃 Amazing shit that happened today:

Have you been kind to yourself
like the way you treat others?
If not, how can you be
kinder to yourself?

There is
nothing in
nature that
blooms all year
long so don't
expect yourself
to do so either

📅 Date:

☀ Daily affirmation - I am fucking:

🧘 I am grateful for:

😎 Things I did for myself today:

😃 Amazing shit that happened today:

What is your **WTF** moment of the year!

📅 Date:

👾 Asshole of the day:

🧘 I am grateful for:

😎 Today, I am proud I didn't:

😃 Amazing shit that happened today:

Joy is
the simplest
form of gratitude
• -Karl Barth •

📅 Date:

☀️ Daily affirmation - I am fucking:

🧘 I am grateful for:

😎 Things I did for myself today:

😃 Amazing shit that happened today:

What are the failures

in life that you

are grateful

for and

why

Gratitude unlocks the fullness of life

📅 Date:

🤪 Asshole of the day:

🧘 I am grateful for:

😎 Today, I am proud
I didn't:

😃 Amazing shit that
happened today:

st out 5 things that would make you feel fucking alive!

It doesn't have to be life changing.

what excites you?

📅 **Date:**

☀ **Daily affirmation - I am fucking:**

🧘 **I am grateful for:**

😎 **Things I did for myself today:**

😃 **Amazing shit that happened today:**

Tell two people today about how grateful you are to have them.

Describe how you feel before and after doing it...

"Feeling gratitude and
not expressing it is like
wrapping a present and
not giving it."

~William Arthur Ward

📅🕐 Date:

😜 Asshole of the day:

🧘 I am grateful for:

😎 Today, I am proud
I didn't:

😃 Amazing shit that
happened today:

Make a list of the funniest thing someone has said to you recently ?

We don't laugh because we're happy,
we're happy because we laugh.
~ William James

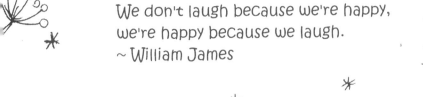

📅🕐 Date:

☀ Daily affirmation - I am fucking:

🧘 I am grateful for:

😎 Things I did for myself today:

😃 Amazing shit that happened today:

BE THANKFUL

FOR WHAT YOU HAVE;
YOU'LL END UP
HAVING MORE.
IF YOU CONCENTRATE
ON WHAT YOU
DON'T HAVE,
YOU WILL NEVER,
EVER HAVE ENOUGH.

-OPRAH WINFREY

📅 Date:

🤪 Asshole of the day:

🧘 I am grateful for:

😎 Today, I am proud
I didn't :

😃 Amazing shit that
happened today:

Is there someone who has hurt or angered you that you need to forgive?

What are the actions that you will take to forgive them?

Forgiveness is the highest, most beautiful form of love. In return, you will receive untold peace and happiness. – Robert Muller

☷🕐 Date:

☀ Daily affirmation - I am fucking:

🧘 I am grateful for:

😎 Things I did for myself today:

😀 Amazing shit that happened today:

What do I think about when you are alone?

You are who you are when
nobody is watching
-Stephen Fry

📅 Date:

😜 Asshole of the day:

🧘 I am grateful for:

😎 Today, I am proud
I didn't:

😃 Amazing shit that
happened today:

What is your **favorite** book, movie, song?
WHY?

📅🕐 **Date:**

☀️ **Daily affirmation - I am fucking:**

🧘 **I am grateful for:**

😎 **Things I did for myself today:**

😃 **Amazing shit that happened today:**

What are your
values in life? And how
have they affected your life?

- John C. Maxwell -
"Your core values are the deeply held beliefs that authentically
describe your soul."

📅🕐 Date:

🐸 Asshole of the day:

🧘 I am grateful for:

😎 Today, I am proud
I didn't:

😃 Amazing shit that
happened today:

My Results

🎯 *What have I achieved so far?*

1. _____

2. _____

3. _____

What have I learned throughout the process?

1. _____

2. _____

3. _____

What have I failed to achieve?

1. _____

2. _____

3. _____

- Why -

_____

_____

_____

Now, look back and be amazed at how much you have changed!

📅🕐 Date:

☀ Daily affirmation - I am fucking:

🧘 I am grateful for:

😎 Things I did for
myself today:

😃 Amazing shit that
happened today:

THE

journey

IS NEVER ENDING.

THERE'S ALWAYS GONNA

be growth, improvement, adversity;

YOU JUST GOTTA

TAKE IT ALL ON

& DO WHAT'S RIGHT.

CONTINUE TO

GROW

Leave an Amazon Review

Take a photo of your personal "Gratitude Journal"

Post & Tag "megumilab" in Instagram and Facebook
to be featured

Stand a chance to win
one of our 10 giveaway sets (per week)
which includes:

o o o o o o o o o o o o o o o o o o o o o o o

ONE $50 Amazon Gift Card

ONE "More Than Yesterday"

ONE "Red Blossom Teacher Planner"

ONE "5-Minute Gratitude Journal"

ONE "2019 Weekly and Monthly Planner"

o o o o o o o o o o o o o o o o o o o o o o o

~ All winners will be contacted through their social media accounts ~

Also by Megumi Lab:

2019 Planner

Red Blossom Teacher Planner

More Than Yesterday –
My Daily Food & Activity
Journal

Good Day Start
With Gratitude
-Gratitude Journal-

~ Preview available at www·megumilab·com ~

About Megumi Lab

TOKYO

Where Does the Name "Megumi" Come From?

Megumi is a Japanese word for "Grace". We believe that with grace, everything beautiful just the way it is. We are founded on grace, evolving through grace, an impacting lives with grace.

Our Mission:

Spread the habit of journaling and be a catalyst for you to listen, feel, and connec with your deeper self.

Our Essence:

At our core, We operate on passion, imagination, love & impact.

Our Promise:

We are obsessively passionate about providing you with the best journaling experience possible. We emphasize simplicity and effectiveness while still maintaining world-class design for all of our products.

Visit us at
Instagram @megumilab
& www.megumilab.com
for more information
regarding our products!

For any inquiries or
questions regarding our
products, please contact us at
megumilabofficial@gmail.com

MEMO

MEMO

37183199R00061

Made in the USA
Lexington, KY
22 April 2019